178274

GRAPHIC NONFICTION

SPARTACUS

THE LIFE OF A ROMAN GLADIATOR

by
ROB SHONE & ANITA GANERI

illustrated by
NICK SPENDER

The Rosen Publishing Group, Inc., New York

Published in 2005 by The Rosen Publishing Group, Inc.
29 East 21st Street, New York, NY 10010

First edition, 2005

Designed and produced by
David West Books

Editor: Gail Bushnell
Photo Research: Carlotta Cooper

Photo credits:
Page 5 – Robert Harding Picture Library
Page 6 (top) – Mary Evans Picture Library
Pages 7 (both) R. Sheridan, 44 (bottom) Prisma, 45 (top) G. T. Garvey – Ancient Art & Architecture Collection Ltd.

Library of Congress Cataloging-in-Publication Data

Shone, Rob.
 Spartacus : the life of a Roman gladiator / by Rob Shone and Anita Ganeri.
 p. cm. — (Graphic nonfiction)
 ISBN 1-4042-0240-4 (lib. bdg.)
 1. Spartacus, d. 71 B.C.—Juvenile literature. 2. Rome—History—Servile Wars,
135–71 B.C.—Juvenile literature. I. Ganeri, Anita. II. Title. III. Series.

 DG258.5.S48 2005
 937'.05'092—dc22

                                                    2004008644

508-4
Bio

Manufactured in China

CONTENTS

WHO'S WHO

 Spartacus (c. 109–71 B.C.) A Thracian slave and gladiator who led a rebellion against the Romans from 73–71 B.C. After many victories, he was finally defeated by Crassus.

 Crixus (??–72 B.C.) A gladiator from Gaul and one of Spartacus's deputies. He was killed by the Romans.

 Marcus Licinius Crassus (112–53 B.C.) A very wealthy Roman general and politician. With Rome's other top generals fighting abroad, Crassus was sent to do battle with Spartacus and put down the slave rebellion.

 Lentulus Batiatus (*dates unknown*) Nothing is known of Lentulus except that he ran a training school for gladiators in Capua, in southern Italy.

 Marcus Porcius (*dates unknown*) A local politician from Pompeii, he paid half of the money for an amphitheater to be built there in 80 B.C.

 Marcus Tullius Cicero (106–43 B.C.) A Roman politician, writer, and lawyer, Cicero was famous for his powerful speeches. Many were written down and tell us a great deal about life in Rome.

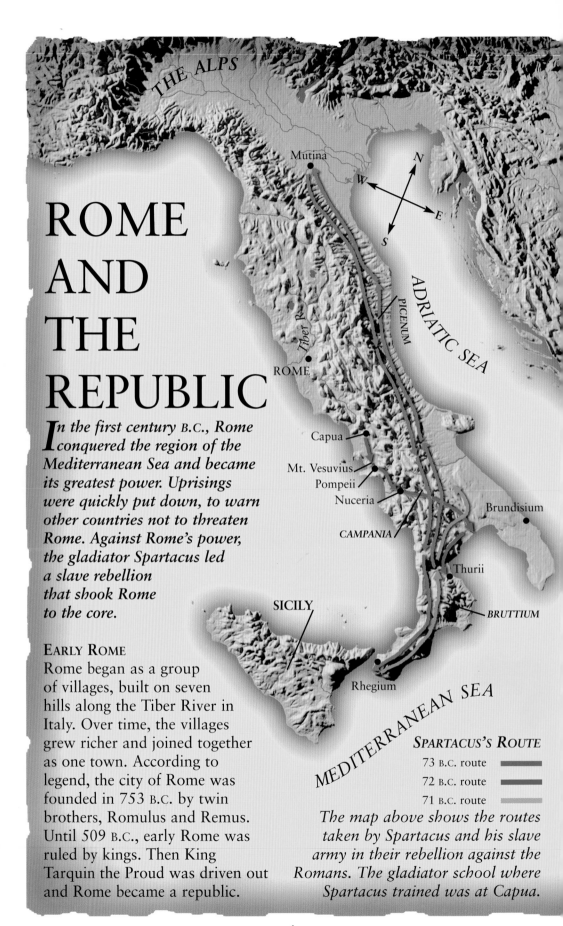

THE ALPS

Mutina

N
W
E
S

ADRIATIC SEA

PICENUM

Tiber R.

ROME

Capua

Mt. Vesuvius
Pompeii
Nuceria

Brundisium

CAMPANIA

Thurii

SICILY

BRUTTIUM

Rhegium

MEDITERRANEAN SEA

ROME AND THE REPUBLIC

*I*n the first century B.C., Rome conquered the region of the Mediterranean Sea and became its greatest power. Uprisings were quickly put down, to warn other countries not to threaten Rome. Against Rome's power, the gladiator Spartacus led a slave rebellion that shook Rome to the core.

EARLY ROME

Rome began as a group of villages, built on seven hills along the Tiber River in Italy. Over time, the villages grew richer and joined together as one town. According to legend, the city of Rome was founded in 753 B.C. by twin brothers, Romulus and Remus. Until 509 B.C., early Rome was ruled by kings. Then King Tarquin the Proud was driven out and Rome became a republic.

SPARTACUS'S ROUTE

73 B.C. route	▬▬▬
72 B.C. route	▬▬▬
71 B.C. route	▬▬▬

The map above shows the routes taken by Spartacus and his slave army in their rebellion against the Romans. The gladiator school where Spartacus trained was at Capua.

Map labels: SPAIN, GAUL, THRACE, ITALY, GREECE, CILICIA, CARTHAGE, MEDITERRANEAN SEA, AFRICA, EGYPT

ROME IN 100 B.C.

By 100 B.C., Rome had conquered many of the lands around the Mediterranean Sea, including Carthage and Greece.

HOME OF THE SENATE

The Forum was a central part of Roman life. It was a group of buildings that served as a marketplace and a meeting place for the Senate.

THE ROMAN REPUBLIC

The Roman republic was governed by a group of officials, called the Senate. The Senate started with 100 senators, but it later had 600. Roman citizens voted each year to elect the senators. Senate affairs and the Roman army were managed by two consuls, the most important government officials. They served in office for one year. Other top officials included eight praetors who acted mainly as judges in the law courts and four *adiles* who looked after public buildings and organized public games.

EXPANSION OF ROME

By 264 B.C., Rome had defeated its Italian neighbors and begun its overseas conquest. The western Mediterranean was controlled by the Carthaginians. The city of Carthage on the north African coast was the center of a great trading empire. In 264 B.C., a series of wars, called the Punic Wars, broke out between Rome and Carthage. Rome beat the Carthaginians and seized their lands. Wars with other powerful states followed. By 50 B.C., most of the Mediterranean had fallen to Rome.

GLADIATORS AND THE GAMES

THE AMPHITHEATER AT POMPEII
The amphitheater at Pompeii was the first to be built in Italy. It held 20,000 people.

*I*n Roman times, people flocked to the public games that were paid for by the government or wealthy citizens. Though gory, the gladiator fights were hugely popular. They were displays of courage and strength, qualities that the Romans greatly admired.

THE GAMES' BEGINNINGS
Gladiator fights were originally held as part of a funeral to honor a dead person's memory. They were put on by the dead person's family. The first contest in Rome took place in 264 B.C., when three pairs of slaves fought in the marketplace. Later, special buildings called amphitheaters were built for the games.

GLADIATORS
Gladiators were mostly criminals, slaves, and prisoners of war. They were trained in special gladiator schools. A successful gladiator might win his freedom. But most had short, brutal lives. They only expected to fight two or three times in the arena before they were killed.

TO LIVE OR DIE?
Gladiators usually fought to the death. A wounded fighter could often ask the crowd to decide if he lived or died.

ANIMALS IN THE ARENA

The gladiators fought in the afternoon and were the main attraction at the games. The entertainment began in the morning, with a procession of gladiators, dancers, and musicians. Next came the wild beast shows. Animals were let loose in the arena to fight each other or attack unarmed prisoners. Wealthy Romans spent vast sums of money shipping beasts such as tigers, bears, and rhinoceroses back to Rome to fight.

BEAST HUNTS
Some animals were put in the arena to be hunted by special gladiators called bestiari. *Thousands of people and animals were killed.*

DAILY SLAVES
Slaves had to look after their masters day and night. In the wall painting above, the slaves are serving their masters at a banquet.

A SLAVE'S LIFE
Rome relied heavily on slave labor. Some slaves were owned by rich Romans. The government also owned slaves. Most of Spartacus's rebel army was made up of runaway slaves who joined the gladiators. Many of the slaves had been prisoners of war and had useful military experience.

TYPES OF GLADIATOR
To make the contest even more exciting, fights were held between different types of gladiators. For example, a retiarius, *armed with a trident and net, might be matched against a* murmillo, *armed with a sword and shield.*

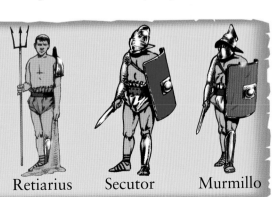

Retiarius   Secutor   Murmillo

SPARTACUS
THE LIFE OF A ROMAN GLADIATOR

73 B.C. IT IS MORNING IN THE TOWN OF POMPEII. THE STREETS ARE UNUSUALLY EMPTY.

OR NEARLY EMPTY...

HURRY UP OR WE'LL MISS THE OPENING PARADE! ARE YOU SURE YOU'VE GOT YOUR TICKET?

YES, UNCLE.

FIRST GAMES, EH? EXCITED?

WELL...

NERVOUS? DON'T WORRY. YOU'LL **LOVE** IT!

SOMEONE ELSE IS IN A HURRY.

YES, DRUSILLA. I'M WELL **AWARE** OF WHAT **CICERO** THINKS.

HE HATES THE GAMES AS MUCH AS YOU DO.

BUT **NOT LIKING** THE GAMES IS SO **UNROMAN!** THE GAMES ARE A SYMBOL OF ROME'S **GREAT POWER** AND **STRENGTH.**

YOU SEE, THE GAMES SHOW US WHAT IT IS TO BE A ROMAN.

OUT OF THE WAY!

OOF!

HEY! WATCH YOURSELF!

CAREFUL, YOU OAF, OR YOU'LL BE CLEANING THE FLOORS USING YOUR OWN SKIN AS A CLOTH!

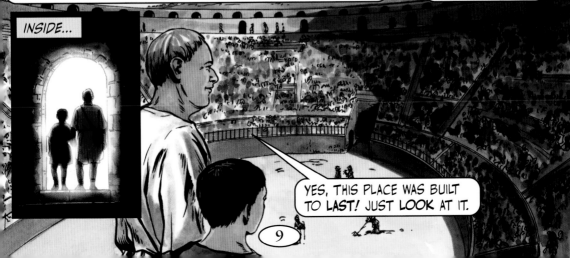

11

THE AFTERNOON'S ENTERTAINMENT...

CUPIDO? HE'S **PATHETIC!** LOOK AT HIM, FIGHTING BY NUMBERS. SLASH, TWO, THREE! THRUST, TWO, THREE! PATHETIC!

CUPIDO! CUPIDO! OOH, ISN'T HE GORGEOUS?

COOEE! CUPIDO! GIVE US A WAVE!

SIXTY SESTERCES ON THE RETIARIUS! WHO'LL TAKE IT?

UH, OH, **TROUBLE.** THE **NUCERIANS** ARE HERE.

DONE!

I THINK HE'S TOO BUSY TO WAVE AT THE MOMENT, LADIES.

IN THE ARENA, A **SECUTOR** FIGHTS A **RETIARIUS**...

SCHICKKK!

THE RETIARIUS SURRENDERS.

BENEATH THE STANDS "MERCURY" AND "CHARON" TALK...

I **HATE** THIS JOB! PEOPLE DON'T RECOGNIZE YOU UNDER ALL THAT PAINT, BUT I'M SICK OF BEING **FOLLOWED** BY KIDS IN THE STREET, CALLING ME NAMES. WE ROMANS CAN BE SO CRUEL AT TIMES!

YEAH, YEAH. LIFE'S TOUGH. IS MY BEARD ON RIGHT?

POMPEIIAN SWINE!

WHO ARE THOSE TWO MEN STANDING NEAR THE GLADIATORS?

NUCERIAN DOG!

THE MAN IN BLACK IS MEANT TO BE CHARON. HE'S COME FROM THE UNDERWORLD, READY TO CLAIM THE DEAD WITH HIS MALLET. THE OTHER ONE IS THE GOD MERCURY. HIS JOB IS TO PROD THE BODY WITH HIS RED-HOT WAND, TO MAKE SURE IT'S DEAD.

KILL! KILL!

AS SPONSOR, MARCUS PORCIUS MUST DECIDE THE RETIARIUS'S FATE...

DEATH!

GGZZZZZ...

OOF! HOW MANY MORE FIGHTS TO GO?

ONLY ONE. IT'S CRIXUS AGAINST THE NEW MAN. A THRACIAN CALLED SPARTACUS.

CRIXUS? WITH TEN WINS TO HIS NAME, THIS WON'T TAKE LONG.

WANT TO HAVE A BET ON IT?

THE THRACIAN WAITS HIS TURN IN THE ARENA.

13

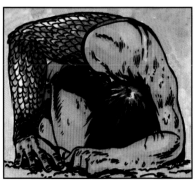

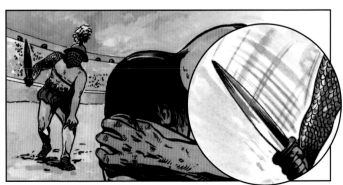

15

GLANGGG!

WHUMPPH!

SPLATTT!

ENOUGH! HE HAS SURRENDERED.

AGAIN, MARCUS PORCIUS MUST DECIDE. THIS TIME, IT IS *LIFE!*

BY EARLY EVENING, THE GAMES ARE OVER.

I THINK THAT ALL WENT RATHER WELL, DRUSILLA DEAR. MARCUS PORCIUS IS INTERESTED IN MY LITTLE BUSINESS VENTURE. AND YOUR MOOD CERTAINLY PICKED UP DURING THE AFTERNOON.

YES, I DID FIND SOME OF THE CONTESTS **INTERESTING**. WHO WAS THAT TALL, BLOND RETIARIUS? AURIUS? HE WAS **VERY** INTERESTING!

DRUSILLA! I'M TAKING YOU HOME, **RIGHT NOW!**

BUT MARCUS PORCIUS IS NOT SO HAPPY...

IT'S A DISASTER! THE CROWD EVEN BOOED ME. TO THINK OF ALL THE MONEY IT COST AND I'LL PROBABLY NOT GET A **SINGLE** VOTE TO SHOW FOR IT. THE LIONS WERE **OLD** AND ALMOST **TOOTHLESS** AND NEARLY ALL THE FIGHTS WERE **DULL** AND **BORING!** AND I KNOW WHO'S TO BLAME – THAT MISERABLE WORM, **LENTULUS BATIATUS**, THE LANISTA! I HATE GLADIATOR OWNERS!

BUT **SURELY**, MARCUS, YOU AND MANY OF YOUR FRIENDS **OWN** GLADIATORS. WHY IS LENTULUS SO **DIFFERENT**?

IT'S NOT THE **SAME**. HE'S A PROFESSIONAL OWNER! WE'RE IN IT FOR THE **FUN!**

OUTSIDE, PEOPLE MAKE THEIR WAY HOME...

WELL, BOY, WHAT DID YOU MAKE OF YOUR FIRST GAMES? IT WASN'T A **CLASSIC**, I GRANT YOU. WHAT IT NEEDED WAS AN **INVENTIVE** TOUCH.

ARE YOU ALRIGHT? YOU'RE VERY **QUIET**.

STILL, I THINK YOU'LL MAKE...

...A GOOD **ROMAN**.

AT HIS GLADIATOR SCHOOL IN *CAPUA*, LENTULUS TALKS TO HIS GLADIATORS...

DULL AND BORING! THOSE WERE MARCUS PORCIUS'S **VERY WORDS!**

HOW MANY TIMES HAVE I TOLD YOU TO STAY AWAY FROM THIS PLACE?

DON'T I TREAT YOU **WELL?** YOU'RE **FED** WHEN YOU'RE HUNGRY AND **CARED FOR** WHEN YOU'RE SICK. THIS IS HOW YOU **REPAY ME!**

HAVE YOU **FORGOTTEN** YOUR SACRED OATH? HAVEN'T I TREATED YOU ALL AS IF YOU WERE MY OWN SONS?

GERMANICUS! SEE TO THAT MAN!

SNICKER!

YES, SIR.

YOUR SPINELESS PERFORMANCE AT POMPEII HAS COST ME **HALF MY FEE!**

HAD A GOOD LAUGH, HAVE WE?

FROM NOW ON, ALL PRIVILEGES ARE **STOPPED.** YOUR HOURS OF TRAINING WILL **DOUBLE** AND FOOD WILL BE **RATIONED** TO MAKE UP FOR ALL THE MONEY I'VE LOST!

PAMPINEUS!

CRIXUS! OH, CRIXUS!

AURIUS, OVER HERE!

AND WILL SOMEONE GET RID OF THOSE **WOMEN** AT THE GATE.

LIFE WAS TOUGH BEFORE. NOW IT IS **UNBEARABLE.**

HOW LONG HAS TITUS BEEN TIED THERE?

TWO DAYS, ALMOST.

PUNISHMENTS ARE CRUEL AND FREQUENT.

AND ALL THAT FOR STEALING A BIT OF MOLDY BREAD.

COMPARED TO THIS SLOP, MOLDY BREAD IS LIKE A FEAST FROM THE GODS!

I'VE GOT A WIFE AND CHILD IN THE TOWN. I'M NOT EVEN ALLOWED TO VISIT THEM.

I GAVE UP MY RIGHTS AS A **FREEBORN CITIZEN** WHEN I DECIDED TO BECOME A GLADIATOR. I DID **NOT** EXPECT TO BE TREATED LIKE SOME **FARMYARD ANIMAL.**

HEY, THRACIAN! I COULD HAVE **KILLED** YOU IN THE ARENA THE OTHER DAY.

WHY **DIDN'T** YOU, CRIXUS?

MOST OF US DIDN'T HAVE THAT CHOICE, ATTALUS.

YOU FOUGHT WELL. YOU DESERVED ANOTHER CHANCE.

WHEN I FIGHT AGAIN, IT'LL BE ON **MY** TERMS.

DANGEROUS TALK, SPARTACUS.

I'LL NOT FIGHT TO ENTERTAIN LAZY ROMANS.

WHAT ARE YOU GOING TO DO?

YOU'LL SEE.

SPARTACUS BEGINS TO FORM A PLAN OF ESCAPE...

...HE WATCHES...

...AND LISTENS...

...SEARCHING OUT THE WEAK SPOTS.

FINALLY, HE IS READY.

IS EVERYONE IN, CRIXUS?

YES.

WE GO TONIGHT. YOU ALL KNOW WHAT TO DO.

SNOK

YOU STUPID OX, CRIXUS! TAKE HIM TO THE HOSPITAL.

IN THE HOSPITAL, SECURITY IS NOT TIGHT. WHY BOTHER TO GUARD SICK MEN SO CLOSELY?

COME ON!

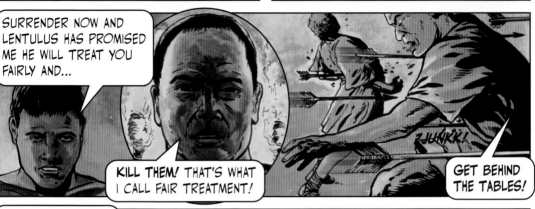

UP THE STAIRS!

IT SHOULD BE ABOUT – HERE!

KLANNGG

THE GUARDS AND LOCAL SOLDIERS ARE NO MATCH FOR THE ARMED GLADIATORS.

THESE SHOULD HELP US!

OVER THE NEXT FEW DAYS, THEIR NUMBER GROWS AS THEY ARE JOINED BY RUNAWAY SLAVES.

WHERE TO NOW, SPARTACUS?

MOUNT VESUVIUS, CRIXUS.

THE REBELS HEAD OUT INTO THE COUNTRYSIDE. THEY CAUSE **PANIC** AMONG THE LOCAL PEOPLE.

MY ARMS ARE STILL ACHING FROM ALL **YOUR** PACKING!

DRUSILLA, IT'S HARDLY **MY** FAULT ALL OUR SLAVES HAVE RUN AWAY. I DIDN'T START THE TROUBLE. BESIDES WE'LL FEEL MUCH SAFER IN **ROME**.

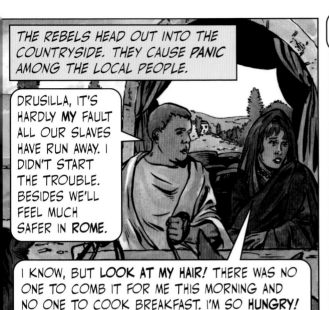

I KNOW, BUT **LOOK AT MY HAIR!** THERE WAS NO ONE TO COMB IT FOR ME THIS MORNING AND NO ONE TO COOK BREAKFAST. I'M SO **HUNGRY!** **AND** I HAD TO DO ALL MY OWN PACKING!

I'VE **ALWAYS** HAD SLAVES AND I HATE **NOT** HAVING THEM. I FEEL SO **POOR!**

I'M BEGINNING TO THINK I SHOULD HAVE LEFT YOU BEHIND FOR YOUR **GLADIATOR BOYFRIEND!**

OTHERS ARE TRYING TO FLEE...

BUT UNCLE, I THOUGHT YOU SAID THAT A GOOD ROMAN ISN'T AFRAID OF ANYTHING, NOT EVEN DEATH.

AND A FAT LOT OF GOOD THIS ROMAN WOULD BE LYING IN A DITCH WITH HIS THROAT CUT. NOW GET ON THE CART, BOY. **WE'RE OFF!**

SUETONIUS PAULINUS! YOU CAN BE SO **CRUDE** AT TIMES!

IN ROME, THE SENATE TAKES A **CALMER** VIEW...

TRUE, OUR FINEST GENERALS AND BEST LEGIONS ARE **ABROAD**. BUT THE TROOPS LEFT AT HOME SHOULD BE MORE THAN ENOUGH TO DESTROY THIS **MOB**.

I SEE NO NEED FOR **ALARM**. WHAT HARM CAN THIS RAGGED ARMY OF THIEVES AND CUTTHROATS DO TO THE **MIGHT** OF ROME?

SOON THEY WILL ALL WISH THEY HAD **DIED** IN THE ARENA.

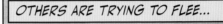

PRAETOR CLAUDIUS GLABER IS GIVEN THE TASK OF SORTING OUT THE TROUBLE IN POMPEII...

WE MUST BE **CAREFUL**, PRAETOR. THE MEN ARE WILLING BUT THEY ARE NEW RECRUITS.

CENTURION, I HAVE 3,000 MEN AGAINST A HANDFUL OF **DISORGANIZED** SLAVES. WHAT IS THERE TO FEAR?

SIR! NEWS FROM VESUVIUS.

ON THE LOWER SLOPES OF MOUNT VESUVIUS...

THEY ARE ON THE TOP OF THE MOUNTAIN. THE **ONLY** WAY DOWN IS ALONG THAT PATH.

EXCELLENT! SOONER OR LATER, THEY WILL HAVE TO COME THROUGH THAT NARROW PASS. WHEN THEY **DO**, WE'LL BE **WAITING!**

THE GLADIATORS' CAMP...

WE'RE **TRAPPED!** WE'LL NEVER GET DOWN THAT WAY. WE'LL ALL BE **KILLED...**

...AND THE CLIFFS ON EITHER SIDE OF US ARE TOO **STEEP** TO CLIMB.

SHORTLY, SLAVES ARE AT WORK ON A QUIET COUNTRY VILLA...

?

THE REBELS! RUN!

SPARTACUS'S SLAVE ARMY MARCHES THROUGH CAMPANIA...

...TAKING ANYTHING THEY WANT.

GET ALL THE HORSES AND ANY WEAPONS AND ARMOR YOU CAN FIND.

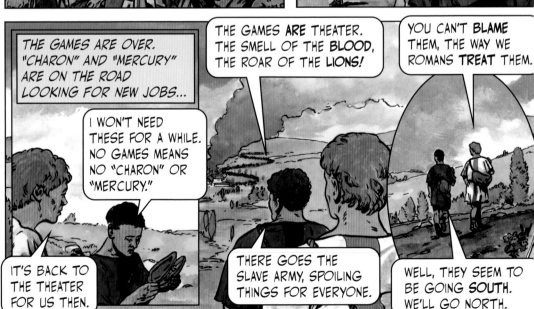

THE GAMES ARE OVER. "CHARON" AND "MERCURY" ARE ON THE ROAD LOOKING FOR NEW JOBS...

I WON'T NEED THESE FOR A WHILE. NO GAMES MEANS NO "CHARON" OR "MERCURY."

IT'S BACK TO THE THEATER FOR US THEN.

THE GAMES ARE THEATER. THE SMELL OF THE BLOOD, THE ROAR OF THE LIONS!

YOU CAN'T BLAME THEM, THE WAY WE ROMANS TREAT THEM.

THERE GOES THE SLAVE ARMY, SPOILING THINGS FOR EVERYONE.

WELL, THEY SEEM TO BE GOING SOUTH. WE'LL GO NORTH.

THE SENATE STAYS CALM AS IT HEARS THE NEWS FROM VESUVIUS. ANOTHER ARMY IS SENT OUT. IT CARRIES THE **FASCES**, AN AX WRAPPED IN A BUNDLE OF REEDS. THIS IS THE SYMBOL OF THE SENATE'S **AUTHORITY** AND OF ROME'S **MIGHT AND POWER**.

THE ROMAN ARMY AND THE REBELS MEET...

DESPITE ALL ITS TRAINING, THE ROMAN ARMY IS NOT PREPARED FOR THE REBELS' FEROCIOUS ATTACK. THE FASCES ARE TAKEN.

SPARTACUS AND HIS ARMY HAVE WON THEIR FIRST VICTORY AGAINST ROME IN OPEN BATTLE.

WHAT ARE YOUR PLANS, SPARTACUS?

IT WILL SOON BE WINTER, CRIXUS. WE MUST FIND SOMEWHERE TO CAMP UNTIL THE SPRING. AFTER THAT, WE HEAD NORTH.

TO ROME?

NO, TO THE **ALPS**. WE'LL CROSS THE MOUNTAINS INTO GAUL, AND **HOME!**

SPARTACUS, WE HAVE **SHOWN** THE SENATE THAT THEIR ARMIES ARE NO MATCH FOR US. WHY STOP? WHY NOT GO TO ROME AND **BRING DOWN** THE REPUBLIC ITSELF? THINK OF **THE RICHES** TO BE HAD THERE.

ROME IS JUST SLEEPING. WE CAUGHT IT BY SURPRISE, THAT'S ALL. BUT IT WILL **SOON WAKE UP** AND COME AFTER US. BY THAT TIME, WE MUST BE FAR AWAY FROM ROME, AND ITALY.

THEN WE GAULS AND GERMANS WILL GO OUR OWN WAY.

SPARTACUS LEADS HIS ARMY OF 70,000 TO THURII IN THE FAR SOUTH. THEY WILL STAY HERE FOR THE WINTER. DISCIPLINE SOON BECOMES A **PROBLEM**...

THEY'VE BEEN FIGHTING OVER THEIR **LOOT**.

WHAT GOOD WILL **GOLD** BE TO THEM WHEN THEY FACE A ROMAN LEGION? HALF THE MEN DON'T HAVE WEAPONS OR ARMOR.

FROM NOW ON, ONLY IRON AND COPPER WILL BE ALLOWED INTO CAMP. FIND SOME BLACKSMITHS. WE HAVE **WEAPONS** TO MAKE.

MEANWHILE, CRIXUS AND HIS GAULS AND GERMANS ARE LIVING THE *GOOD LIFE.*

THE SPRING OF 72 B.C. FINDS THEM NORTH OF THURII.

CRIXUS DOES NOT KNOW IT YET, BUT ROME HAS SENT A NEW ARMY MADE UP OF FOUR LEGIONS TO *FIND* AND **KILL HIM.**

WHILE CRIXUS AND HIS REBELS EAT AND DRINK, CONSUL GELLIUS PUBLICOLA AND TWO OF THE LEGIONS ARE MOVING CLOSE TO CRIXUS'S CAMP...

...VERY CLOSE.

THE ROMANS KILL CRIXUS AND 20,000 OF HIS MEN.

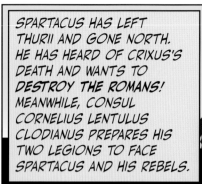

SPARTACUS HAS LEFT THURII AND GONE NORTH. HE HAS HEARD OF CRIXUS'S DEATH AND WANTS TO *DESTROY THE ROMANS!* MEANWHILE, CONSUL CORNELIUS LENTULUS CLODIANUS PREPARES HIS TWO LEGIONS TO FACE SPARTACUS AND HIS REBELS.

HERE THEY COME. I DON'T EXPECT THIS TO TAKE TOO LONG. SEE! THEIR LEFT WING IS ALREADY FALLING BACK.

LOOK! ARE THEY SUPPOSED TO HAVE HORSEMEN? WE HAVE NONE, DO WE?

WHAT?

YOU FOOL! THEY DON'T JUST HAVE HORSEMEN, THEY HAVE A *CAVALRY!* SOUND THE *RETREAT!* THEY'LL HAVE MY *HEAD* IN ROME FOR THIS, IF I'VE STILL GOT ONE!

IN MEMORY OF CRIXUS, SPARTACUS HOLDS GAMES. THE 300 ROMAN PRISONERS ARE THE GLADIATORS. THEY ARE **FORCED** TO FIGHT EACH OTHER TO THE DEATH.

HOW DID YOU MANAGE TO TRICK THE ROMANS, SPARTACUS? IT'S AS IF YOU **THINK** LIKE THEM.

I WAS ONE OF THEM **ONCE**. I **SERVED** IN THEIR ARMY AS A **SOLDIER**.

WHAT HAPPENED?

I RAN AWAY BUT THEY CAUGHT ME AND MADE ME A GLADIATOR. YES, I KNOW THE ROMANS.

MARCHING NORTH, SPARTACUS BRUSHES ASIDE AN ATTACK BY A ROMAN ARMY AT PICENUM AND ANOTHER ATTACK AT MUTINA.

IN ROME, POLITICIAN MARCUS CICERO IS ENTERTAINING GUESTS...

THEY'VE BEEN **FRIGHTENING** THE COUNTRY FOR NEARLY **TWO YEARS!** THERE'S HARDLY AN ESTATE IN CENTRAL ITALY THAT THOSE THIEVES HAVEN'T VISITED! AND THINK OF ALL THE SLAVES THEY'VE **FREED** AND ALL THE TREASURES THEY'VE **TAKEN!**

IT WOULD SEEM WE ARE **POWERLESS** TO STOP THEM, CICERO! THEY HAVE TURNED US ALL INTO LAUGHINGSTOCKS.

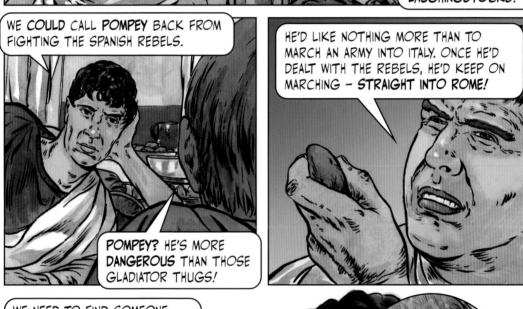

WE **COULD** CALL **POMPEY** BACK FROM FIGHTING THE SPANISH REBELS.

HE'D LIKE NOTHING MORE THAN TO MARCH AN ARMY INTO ITALY. ONCE HE'D DEALT WITH THE REBELS, HE'D KEEP ON MARCHING – **STRAIGHT INTO ROME!**

POMPEY? HE'S MORE **DANGEROUS** THAN THOSE GLADIATOR THUGS!

WE NEED TO FIND SOMEONE **LESS HEADSTRONG** BUT JUST AS FIERCE AND **EXPERIENCED.**

WHAT ABOUT **MARCUS CRASSUS?**

MARCUS CRASSUS? YES. HE'S **CLEVER** AND HE HAS LED SOLDIERS IN BATTLE. HE IS ALSO VERY **RICH** AND COULD EVEN **AFFORD TO PAY** FOR AN ARMY.

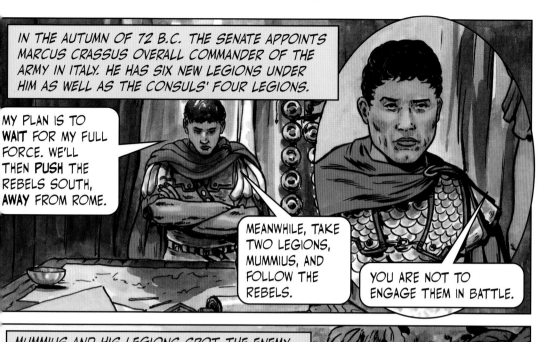

IN THE AUTUMN OF 72 B.C. THE SENATE APPOINTS MARCUS CRASSUS OVERALL COMMANDER OF THE ARMY IN ITALY. HE HAS SIX NEW LEGIONS UNDER HIM AS WELL AS THE CONSULS' FOUR LEGIONS.

MY PLAN IS TO **WAIT** FOR MY FULL FORCE. WE'LL THEN **PUSH** THE REBELS SOUTH, **AWAY** FROM ROME.

MEANWHILE, TAKE TWO LEGIONS, MUMMIUS, AND FOLLOW THE REBELS.

YOU ARE NOT TO ENGAGE THEM IN BATTLE.

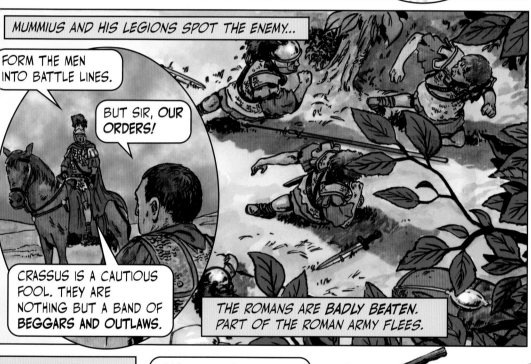

MUMMIUS AND HIS LEGIONS SPOT THE ENEMY...

FORM THE MEN INTO BATTLE LINES.

BUT SIR, OUR ORDERS!

CRASSUS IS A CAUTIOUS FOOL. THEY ARE NOTHING BUT A BAND OF **BEGGARS AND OUTLAWS.**

THE ROMANS ARE **BADLY BEATEN.** PART OF THE ROMAN ARMY FLEES.

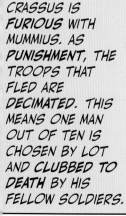

CRASSUS IS **FURIOUS** WITH MUMMIUS. AS **PUNISHMENT,** THE TROOPS THAT FLED ARE **DECIMATED.** THIS MEANS ONE MAN OUT OF TEN IS CHOSEN BY LOT AND **CLUBBED TO DEATH** BY HIS FELLOW SOLDIERS.

THEY WILL LEARN TO **FEAR ME** MORE THAN THEY FEAR THE REBELS.

CRASSUS'S ARMY GRADUALLY FORCES THE REBELS SOUTH TO BRUTTIUM.

THEY HAVE **NOWHERE** TO GO NOW. I WANT TO **KEEP** IT THAT WAY.

THE ROMANS BUILD A WALL AND A DITCH. IT TRAPS THE REBELS IN SOUTHERN ITALY.

IT STRETCHES FROM COAST TO COAST.

MEANWHILE, AT THE SOUTHERN TIP OF MAINLAND ITALY...

WE JUST NEED TO GET TO **SICILY.** IT WON'T TAKE MUCH TO SPARK A **NEW REBELLION.**

CRUCIFIED? AN INNOCENT ROMAN CITIZEN? A SHAMEFUL DEATH – SHAMEFUL FOR ROME!

WHERE WILL THESE BARBARIAN DEVILS STOP? ON THE HILLS OF **ROME**?

DO YOU KNOW HOW MANY GLADIATORS, LET ALONE SLAVES, ARE CURRENTLY IN ROME? **THOUSANDS!** WHAT DO YOU THINK WOULD HAPPEN IF THEY ALL CAUGHT THIS **FREEDOM DISEASE**?

WE MUST SEND FOR POMPEY AND CALL LICINIUS LUCULLUS AND HIS LEGIONS BACK FROM MACEDONIA IN THE EAST. THE DANGER TO ROME IS TOO GREAT.

BUT SPARTACUS'S MEN NEED FOOD AND SUPPLIES. THEY MUST BREAK THROUGH THE ROMAN WALL. THEY HAVE TESTED THE ROMAN GUARDS ALL ALONG ITS VAST LENGTH, LOOKING FOR WEAK POINTS. NOW, THEY DARE NOT FAIL.

WHAT A FILTHY NIGHT! WHEN DO WE GO OFF DUTY?

ABOUT AN HOUR.

DID YOU HEAR SOMETHING?

IT'S JUST THE WIND.

NO, THERE IT GOES AGAIN!

SOUND THE ALARM!

CRASSUS IS NOT HAPPY. NOT ONLY HAVE SPARTACUS AND MOST OF HIS MEN ESCAPED, BUT HE ALSO HEARS THE NEWS FROM ROME. POMPEY HAS BEEN SENT FOR.

I WILL NOT ALLOW POMPEY TO STEAL VICTORY FROM ME! MY VICTORY!

WE MUST FOLLOW THE REBELS AND FORCE THEM TO FIGHT. I HAVE TO BEAT THEM, BEFORE POMPEY DOES!

IT IS 71 B.C. SPARTACUS FLEES EAST AS FAST AS HE CAN. HE HOPES TO GET TO **BRUNDISIUM** ON THE COAST. THEN BAD NEWS ARRIVES. LUCULLUS AND HIS ARMY ARE BACK FROM MACEDONIA AND HAVE LANDED ON THE EAST COAST. THE WAY FORWARD IS **BLOCKED.**

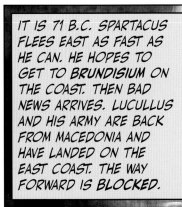

WE HAVE AN ARMY IN **FRONT** OF US, CRASSUS CHASING FROM BEHIND, AND POMPEY TO THE **NORTH.** WE CAN DO NO MORE. WE **STAND** AND **FIGHT.**

IN SOUTHERN CAMPANIA, SPARTACUS'S ARMY TURNS AROUND, FORMS INTO BATTLE LINES, AND WAITS FOR CRASSUS.

AT LAST! THEY WISH TO FIGHT IN OPEN BATTLE.

THE BATTLE BECOMES A **MASSACRE**. SOME REBELS MANAGE TO ESCAPE NORTH WHERE POMPEY'S ARMY IS WAITING. NONE SURVIVE. SPARTACUS'S BODY IS **NEVER FOUND**.

THE ROMANS TAKE 6,000 REBEL PRISONERS. THEY ARE **CRUCIFIED** ALONG THE **APPIAN WAY**, WHICH RUNS FROM CAPUA TO ROME. ONE CAPTIVE HANGS EVERY 30 YARDS FOR 200 MILES.

FAMILY! THEY WERE LIKE **FAMILY** TO ME, GERMANICUS! NOW THE GOOD NAME LENTULUS BATIATUS ISN'T WORTH A LEAD SESTERCE. WE CAN'T STAY IN ITALY.

KERLIP
KERLOP

I'VE HEARD THE GAMES ARE POPULAR IN THE PROVINCES. PERHAPS WE SHOULD GO TO SPAIN, OR EVEN AFRICA? WE'D BE CLOSE TO A READY SUPPLY OF SLAVES AND WILD BEASTS AND FREE FROM INTERFERING BUSYBODIES. HMM, **AFRICA!**

ROME FINDS IT HAS NEW PROBLEMS. BOTH POMPEY AND CRASSUS ARE CLAIMING VICTORY OVER THE REBELS. NEITHER WILL LET HIS ARMY GO. IF A SOLUTION IS NOT FOUND, IT WILL MEAN **CIVIL WAR**...

LET POMPEY HAVE HIS VICTORY PARADE THROUGH ROME, CRASSUS, NOT FOR HIS SMALL PART IN DEFEATING THE REBELS BUT FOR HIS SPANISH CAMPAIGN. AFTER ALL, WHERE IS THE GLORY IN BEATING A FEW THOUSAND CRIMINALS? STAND YOUR ARMY DOWN AND FORM AN ALLIANCE WITH HIM. ROME WILL BE **ETERNALLY GRATEFUL TO YOU.**

WISE WORDS. I WILL GAIN MORE FOR SEEMING TO BE A PEACEMAKER THAN A WARMONGER. I CAN SEE YOU MAY RISE TO GREAT HEIGHTS ONE DAY, **GAIUS JULIUS CAESAR.**

BY THE AUTUMN, LIFE IS BACK TO NORMAL. MEANWHILE, IN THE AMPHITHEATER AT POMPEII...

SO, HERE WE ARE AGAIN FOR ANOTHER DAY OF FUN, THRILLS, AND SPILLS.

DO YOU THINK THE GAMES HAVE A **FUTURE?**

MARCUS PORCIUS!

OF COURSE! LISTEN TO THAT ROAR. DEATH SELLS.

IF WE'RE **CLEVER**, WE'VE GOT A JOB FOR LIFE.

MARCUS PORCIUS!

CAREFUL!

MARCUS PORCIUS! WAIT!

OH, IT'S **YOU**, PAULINUS. WHAT DO YOU WANT?

I'VE HEARD OF ANOTHER GOLDEN BUSINESS OPPORTUNITY THAT MAY...

WAIT, I'VE LOST AN EAR!

STOP! I LOST ENOUGH MONEY ON THAT GLADIATOR **SCHEME** OF YOURS.

BUT I'M FORGETTING MY MANNERS. HOW IS YOUR CHARMING WIFE? DRUSILLA, ISN'T IT?

WE DIVORCED.

I CAN'T GO INTO THE ARENA WITH ONLY ONE EAR! HELP ME FIND IT!

AS I'M SURE YOU KNEW! GLADIATORS!

OUT OF MY WAY!

WATCH YOURSELF!

WHAT'S THAT ON THE FLOOR?

LOOK LAD, WE'VE BEEN TO THE GAMES **EVERY DAY** THIS WEEK! THERE ARE OTHER THINGS IN LIFE.

...A GOOD ROMAN?

LOOK, IT'S "ONE EAR" CHARON!

SIGH!

THE RETIARIUS! HE'S DONE FOR! KILL HIM! **KILL HIM! KILL!**

BUT UNCLE, DON'T YOU WANT ME TO BECOME...

FOR THE NEXT 470 YEARS, GLADIATORS WILL FIGHT AND DIE IN THE ROMAN ARENAS FOR THE ENJOYMENT OF ALL *GOOD ROMANS*.

THE END

AFTER THE REVOLT

Although Spartacus's uprising was finally crushed, it had been a warning to the Romans. The Senate had not taken the rebels seriously enough and many Romans had been killed in the fighting. Rome was determined that this sort of threat to its power would never happen again.

THE COLOSSEUM
Opened in A.D. 80, the Colosseum in Rome was the greatest amphitheater in the Roman Empire. This vast building had room for about 50,000 people.

AFTERMATH

After Spartacus's uprising, several other groups of gladiators tried to rebel. These revolts did not last long and were quickly put down by the Romans. To make sure that the revolts stopped, the Romans applied stricter discipline at the gladiator schools. The gladiators were closely supervised and the stores of weapons carefully guarded.

AN UNEASY PEACE

After putting down the slave rebellion, Pompey and Crassus joined forces and demanded to be made consuls. They were elected in 70 B.C. In 60 B.C., Pompey and Crassus formed an alliance with Julius Caesar against their political rivals, a group of senators called *optimates*. Caesar was elected consul in 59 B.C.

JULIUS CAESAR

Julius Caesar (c. 100–44 B.C.) was a brilliant soldier and politician. Caesar led his armies into Spain, Gaul, and Britain before returning to Rome to take power.

CIVIL WAR

In 53 B.C., Crassus was killed in battle and the alliance began to break up. With Caesar away in Gaul, or modern-day France, the Senate persuaded Pompey to become consul. The *optimates* were worried that Caesar would return to Rome and challenge their authority. Civil war broke out between Caesar and Pompey, who was backed by the *optimates*. In 49 B.C., however, Caesar led his army into Rome and seized power. Over the next few years, he defeated Pompey's armies in Spain, Greece, and Africa.

THE END OF THE REPUBLIC

Following his victories, Caesar was made dictator for life. Caesar introduced popular social reforms, but many senators felt that he threatened their power. He was murdered on March 15, 44 B.C. Civil wars broke out and the republic ended. In 27 B.C., Caesar's adopted son, Octavian, defeated his rivals to become leader of the Roman world. He took the name "Augustus" and became the first Roman emperor.

POMPEY THE GREAT
The powerful Roman general Pompey (106–48 B.C.) was called back from fighting in Spain to help Crassus crush Spartacus's rebellion. Pompey was later elected consul.

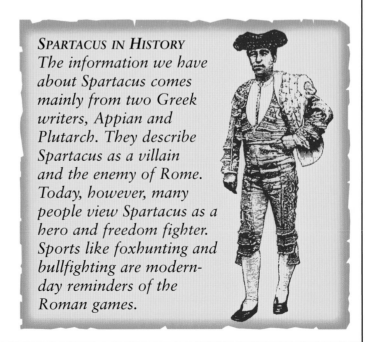

SPARTACUS IN HISTORY
The information we have about Spartacus comes mainly from two Greek writers, Appian and Plutarch. They describe Spartacus as a villain and the enemy of Rome. Today, however, many people view Spartacus as a hero and freedom fighter. Sports like foxhunting and bullfighting are modern-day reminders of the Roman games.

GLOSSARY

alliance An agreement to work together.

amphitheater A circular or oval building in which gladiator fights were held.

Appian Way The first major road to be built in Rome. It ran from Rome to Capua.

arena A large area used for sports or entertainment.

cavalry Soldiers who fight on horseback.

centurion An officer in the Roman army who commanded a unit of 100 men.

Charon The boatman who ferried people's souls across the Styx River to the Underworld.

consul The most senior official in the Roman government. Two consuls were elected each year.

crucified To put someone to death by nailing to a cross.

decimate To select by lot and kill every tenth man; to destroy a large part of something.

discipline Control over the way someone thinks or behaves.

execution The killing of someone for a crime.

Gauls People who lived in what is now France.

legion A 5,000-man unit of the Roman army.

massacre The brutal killing of a large number of people.

murmillo A gladiator who fought with a sword and shield.

Nucerians People from the city of Nuceria, east of Pompeii.

oath A serious, formal promise.

praetor A senior official in the Roman government.

province An outlying area of a country, away from the center of population.

ration To give out in limited amounts.

rebellion A struggle against the people in charge of something.

recruits People who have recently joined an army or organization.

republic A country or state in which the people elect representatives who manage the government.

retiarius A gladiator who fought with a net and a trident.

secutor A gladiator who fought with a sword and shield, often chasing his opponent, who would normally be a *retiarius*.

Senate The group of officials which governed Rome. These officials were called senators.

sesterces Units of Roman currency.

sponsor Someone who gives money to support the work of others.

Thracian A person from Thrace, or what is now Bulgaria.

trident A long, three-pronged spear.

FOR MORE
INFORMATION

ORGANIZATIONS

The Metropolitan Museum of Art
1000 Fifth Avenue
New York, NY 10028-0198
(212) 535-7710
Web site: http://www.metmuseum.org/

Virginia Museum of Fine Arts
200 N. Boulevard
Richmond, VA 23220-4007
(804) 340-1400
Web site: http://www.vmfa.state.va.us/

FOR FURTHER READING

Brown, Dale, ed. *Rome: Echoes of Imperial Glory*. Boston, MA:
Time-Life, Inc., 1999.

Corbishley, Mike. *Ancient Rome*. New York: Facts On File Inc., 2003.

Fast, Howard. *Spartacus*. Armonk, NY: M. E. Sharpe, Inc., 1996.

Marks, Anthony, and Graham Tingay. *The Romans*. Tulsa, OK: EDC
Publishing, 1990.

Nardo, Don. *Life of a Roman Gladiator*. Farmington Hills, MI: Gale
Group, 2003.

Nardo, Don. *The Roman Colosseum*. Farmington Hills, MI: Gale
Group, 2001.

Watkins, Richard Ross. *Gladiator*. Wilmington, MA: Houghton Mifflin
Company Trade & Reference Division, 1997.

INDEX

Web Sites

Due to the changing nature of Internet links, the Rosen Publishing Group, Inc., has developed an online list of Web sites related to the subject of this book. This site is updated regularly. Please use this link to access the list:

http://www.rosenlinks.com/gnf/sparta